DEAR BO AND MARGOT

May this little booklet be a source of love, strength and encouragement for the future. Eternity is forever.

Love,

Kane.

*Copyright © 1977 Lion Publishing
121 High Street, Berkhamsted, Herts*

*First edition 1976
Reprinted 1977, 1978*

U.S.A. Edition, Published By
*David C. Cook Publishing Co.
Elgin IL 60120*

ISBN 0-89191-123-5

Photographs by David Alexander, pages 7, 9 (and cover), 11, 13, 15, 19, 21, 25, 27, 29, 31, 33, 35, 39, 43, 45; Michael Richards (RSPB), page 17; Fritz Fankhauser, page 23; Jean-Luc Ray, pages 37, 41

Quotations from Good News Bible, Today's English Version, *copyright 1966, 1971 and 1976 American Bible Society; by permission of the British and Foreign Bible Society.*

Printed in Great Britain by Purnell and Sons Ltd, Paulton

A word of promise

GOD'S WORD WILL PROSPER

My word is like the snow and the rain
that come down from the sky
to water the earth.
They make the crops grow
and provide seed for sowing and food to eat.
So also will be the word that I speak—
it will not fail to do what I plan for it;
it will do everything I send it to do.

You will leave Babylon with joy;
you will be led out of the city in peace.
The mountains and hills will burst into
singing,
and the trees will shout for joy.

ISAIAH 55: 10-12

'NOAH SENT OUT A DOVE'

God said to Noah and his sons,
'I am now making my covenant with you and with your descendants, and with all living beings—all birds and all animals—everything that came out of the boat with you . . .

'As a sign of this everlasting covenant which I am making with you and with all living beings, I am putting my bow in the clouds. It will be the sign of my covenant with the world . . .

'Never again will I put the earth under a curse because of what man does . . . Never again will I destroy all living beings, as I have done this time. As long as the world exists, there will be a time for planting and a time for harvest. There will always be cold and heat, summer and winter, day and night.'

GENESIS 9: 8-10, 12-13; 8: 21-22

'LOOK HOW THE WILD FLOWERS GROW'

I tell you not to worry about the food you need to stay alive or about the clothes you need for your body. Life is much more important than food, and the body much more important than clothes . . .

Can any of you live a bit longer by worrying about it? If you can't manage even such a small thing, why worry about the other things?

Look how the wild flowers grow: they don't work or make clothes for themselves. But I tell you that not even King Solomon with all his wealth had clothes as beautiful as one of these flowers. It is God who clothes the wild grass . . .

So don't be all upset, always concerned about what you will eat and drink . . . Your Father knows that you need these things. Instead, be concerned with his Kingdom, and he will provide you with these things.

LUKE 12: 22, 25-31

I WILL SEEK THE LOST

'I, the Sovereign Lord, tell you that I myself will look for my sheep and take care of them . . .

'I myself will be the shepherd of my sheep, and I will find them a place to rest. I, the Sovereign Lord, have spoken.

'I will look for those that are lost, bring back those that wander off, bandage those that are hurt, and heal those that are sick . . .

'You, my sheep, the flock that I feed, are my people, and I am your God,' says the Sovereign Lord.

EZEKIEL 34: 11, 15-16, 31

JUSTICE FOR THE POOR

The royal line of David is like a tree that has been cut down; but just as new branches sprout from a stump, so a new king will arise from among David's descendants.

The spirit of the Lord will give him wisdom, and the knowledge and skill to rule his people.
He will know the Lord's will and honour him, and find pleasure in obeying him.
He will not judge by appearance or hearsay; he will judge the poor fairly
and defend the rights of the helpless.

ISAIAH 11: 1-4

NOT FORGOTTEN

Aren't five sparrows sold for two pennies?
Yet not one sparrow is forgotten by God.
Even the hairs of your head have all been
counted. So do not be afraid; you are worth
much more than many sparrows!

LUKE 12: 6-7

RIVERS AND SPRINGS

When my people in their need look for water,
when their throats are dry with thirst,
then I, the Lord, will answer their prayer;
I, the God of Israel, will never abandon them.
I will make rivers flow among barren hills
and springs of water run in the valleys.
I will turn the desert into pools of water
and the dry land into flowing springs.
I will make cedars grow in the desert,
and acacias and myrtles and olive-trees.
Forests will grow in barren land,
forests of pine and juniper and cypress.
People will see this and know
that I, the Lord, have done it.
They will come to understand
that Israel's holy God has made it happen.

ISAIAH 41 : 17-20

LEAVING HOME AND FAMILY

Jesus said:
'I tell you that anyone who leaves home or brothers or sisters or mother or father or children or fields for me and for the gospel, will receive much more in this present age. He will receive a hundred times more houses, brothers, sisters, mothers, children and fields —and persecutions as well; and in the age to come he will receive eternal life.'

MARK 10: 29-30

SET FREE FROM PRISON

The Lord says,
'Here is my servant, whom I strengthen—
the one I have chosen, with whom I am pleased.
I have filled him with my spirit,
and he will bring justice to every nation.
He will not shout or raise his voice
or make loud speeches in the streets.
He will not break off a bent reed
or put out a flickering lamp.
He will bring lasting justice to all.
He will not lose hope or courage;
he will establish justice on the earth.
Distant lands eagerly wait for his teaching . . .'

Now the Lord God says to his servant,
'I, the Lord, have called you and given you power
to see that justice is done on earth.
Through you I will make a covenant with all peoples;
through you I will bring light to the nations.
You will open the eyes of the blind
and set free those who sit in dark prisons.'

ISAIAH 42: 1-7

'ALL WILL KNOW ME'

The Lord says,
'The time is coming when I will make a new covenant with the people of Israel and with the people of Judah. It will not be like the old covenant that I made with their ancestors when I took them by the hand and led them out of Egypt. Although I was like a husband to them, they did not keep that covenant.

'The new covenant that I will make with the people of Israel will be this: I will put my law within them and write it on their hearts. I will be their God, and they will be my people. None of them will have to teach his fellow-countryman to know the Lord, because all will know me, from the least to the greatest. I will forgive their sins and I will no longer remember their wrongs. I, the Lord, have spoken.'

JEREMIAH 31: 31-34

WATER FOR A THIRSTY LAND

'I am the God who forgives your sins,
and I do this because of who I am.
I will not hold your sins against you . . .'

The Lord says,
'Listen now, Israel, my servant,
my chosen people, the descendants of Jacob.
I am the Lord who created you;
from the time you were born, I have helped you.
Do not be afraid; you are my servant,
my chosen people whom I love.

'I will give water to the thirsty land
and make streams flow on the dry ground.
I will pour out my power on your children
and my blessing on your descendants.
They will thrive like well-watered grass,
like willows by streams of running water.

'One by one, people will say, "I am the Lord's."
They will come to join the people of Israel.
Each one will mark the name of the Lord on his arm
and call himself one of God's people.'

ISAIAH 43: 25; 44: 1-5

THE WINDOWS OF HEAVEN

'Turn back to me, and I will turn to you.
But you ask, "What must we do to turn
back to you?"
I ask you, is it right for a person to cheat
God? Of course not, yet you are cheating me.
"How?" you ask.
In the matter of tithes and offerings. A
curse is on all of you because the whole
nation is cheating me. Bring the full amount
of your tithes to the Temple, so that there
will be plenty of food there. Put me to the
test and you will see that I will open the
windows of heaven and pour out on you in
abundance all kinds of good things.'

MALACHI 3: 7-10

MY SHEEP

Jesus said:
'My sheep listen to my voice; I know them, and they follow me. I give them eternal life, and they shall never die. No one can snatch them away from me. What my Father has given me is greater than everything, and no one can snatch them away from the Father's care. The Father and I are one.'

JOHN 10: 27-30

'I WILL LEAD...'

I will lead my blind people
by roads they have never travelled.
I will turn their darkness into light
and make rough country smooth before them.
These are my promises,
and I will keep them without fail.

ISAIAH 42: 16

'PEACE I GIVE YOU'

When I go, you will not be left all alone;
I will come back to you. In a little while the
world will see me no more, but you will see
me; and because I live, you also will live . . .

I have told you this while I am still with you.
The Helper, the Holy Spirit, whom the
Father will send in my name, will teach you
everything, and make you remember all that
I have told you.

Peace is what I leave with you; it is my own
peace that I give you. I do not give it as the
world does. Do not be worried and upset; do
not be afraid. You heard me say to you,
'I am leaving, but I will come back to you.'

JOHN 14: 18-19, 25-28

IF YOU ASK...

I am telling you the truth: whoever believes in me will do what I do—yes, he will do even greater things, because I am going to the Father. And I will do whatever you ask for in my name, so that the Father's glory will be shown through the Son. If you ask me for anything in my name, I will do it.

JOHN 14: 12-14

THEY LIVED IN TENTS

By faith Abraham lived as a foreigner in the country that God had promised him, as though he were a foreigner. He lived in tents, as did Isaac and Jacob, who received the same promise from God. For Abraham was waiting for the city which God has designed and built, the city with permanent foundations . . .

It was in faith that all these persons died. They did not receive the things God had promised, but from a long way off they saw and welcomed them, and admitted openly that they were foreigners and refugees on earth. Those who say such things make it clear that they are looking for a country of their own. They did not keep thinking about the country they had left; if they had, they would have had the chance to return. Instead, it was a better country they longed for, the heavenly country. And so God is not ashamed for them to call him their God, because he has prepared a city for them.

HEBREWS 11: 9-10, 13-16

'HOW HAPPY I AM'

How happy I am because of your promises—
as happy as someone who finds rich treasure.

PSALM 119: 162

LIVING TOGETHER IN PEACE

Wolves and sheep will live together in peace,
and leopards will lie down with young goats.
Calves and lion cubs will feed together,
and little children will take care of them.
Cows and bears will eat together,
and their calves and cubs will lie down in peace.
Lions will eat straw as cattle do.
Even a baby will not be harmed
if it plays near a poisonous snake.
On Zion, God's sacred hill,
there will be nothing harmful or evil.
The land will be as full of knowledge of the Lord
as the seas are full of water.

A day is coming when the new king from the royal line of David will be a symbol to the nations. They will gather in his royal city and give him honour.

ISAIAH 11:6-10

'I WILL BE WITH YOU ALWAYS'

Jesus drew near and said to them:
'I have been given all authority in heaven
and on earth. Go, then, to all peoples
everywhere and make them my disciples:
baptize them in the name of the Father,
the Son, and the Holy Spirit, and teach them
to obey everything I have commanded you.
And I will be with you always, to the end
of the age.'

MATTHEW 28: 18-20